Venus Envy

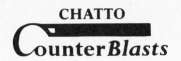

CHATTO
CounterBlasts

Adam
MARS-JONES

Venus Envy

Chatto & Windus
LONDON

Published in 1990 by
Chatto & Windus Ltd
20 Vauxhall Bridge Road
London SW1V 2SA

A CIP catalogue record for this book
is available from the British Library

ISBN 0 7011 3585 9

The publishers wish to thank Alasdair Gray and
Jonathan Cape Ltd for permission to reproduce the
excerpt from *1982, Janine* which appears on pages 36–7.

Photoset in Linotron Ehrhardt by
Rowland Phototypesetting Ltd
Bury St Edmunds, Suffolk
Printed in Great Britain by
St Edmundsbury Press Ltd
Bury St Edmunds, Suffolk

IN THESE PAGES a spirit notorious for its mildness must summon up the necessary unfairness of polemic. Can I bloat my little grievance to impressive size? I must try. I must aim to be worthy of the price paid for paper and ink, by every squeezed octopus and melted tree.

Hobbyhorse, where are you? Come and be saddled. I see you there, lurking in the shadows of the stable block. The sunlight catches your long lashes, as they graze the slickness of your eyeball. Come from the shadows. Come and be saddled.

You are delicate, almost neurotic in your prancing. You sidle towards me, you push your muzzle of moist ultrasuede against my leg. Up close, your mane looks to be blow-dried – scrunch-permed, even. Worse, you are knee-high. Are you then *Eohippus*, the Dawn Horse, tiny ancestor of all the modern breeds, strumming a simpler planet with your foreshortened hoofs? No. You are plastic, you are pink and lilac. Are you in fact that bane of the tasteful parent, pastel nightmare that haunts Christmas lists – though any sensible Santa would hack you into rough steaks to feed the reindeer – My Little Pony? No matter. We must ride.

Feminism has changed the way men think but not in the way that feminists might have hoped. Although feminist criticism has made some male habits unfashionable in certain circles, masculinity has been quick to redefine itself, in terms not of nature or even of freedom, but in terms of responsibility. Lost ground has been recaptured, without any admission that ground was lost in the first place, or that any slow struggle is going on. A new style has arisen of faintly synthetic introspection, presented as a maturing process unprompted by contemporary debates, which nevertheless reads more convincingly as a rhetorical response to cultural pressure.

This is a subject of more than passing interest. A lot depends on how our culture comes to terms with the idea of its own destructiveness, an idea that can't be ignored indefinitely but is likely to appear in the form of bargains and wishful evasions. The longer these bargains are received uncritically, the less likely it is that we will make real changes in our behaviour.

This essay will examine how the redefinition has been accomplished, in two books of fiction published in the late eighties: *Einstein's Monsters* by Martin Amis and *The Child in Time* by Ian McEwan. Apologies to these two gentlemen for seizing on their work of that period as exemplary, apologies also to everyone else. If there's one thing more annoying than being singled out for analysis in a wide-ranging, witty, provocative essay on profound cultural change, it's being passed over by same.

I make no apology – is there a more defensive phrase in the language? – for analysing literature rather than softer material (newspaper articles, adver-

2

tisements). A book of fiction is a very concentrated piece of mental behaviour. It is highly self-conscious, but it can also have the paradoxical property of shielding an author from his opinions, allowing them to develop independently. These books are also quite good enough to set up a sort of defensive force-field, a crackling barrier that throws off flimsy speculations, making them look as foolish as they are.

And if writers of this quality can't engage with the major issues of life without including a disabling amount of propaganda on behalf of their gender, how much can be expected of anyone else?

(Memo to self: praise in an essay like this sounds fishy, hypocritical. No more of it. Sensible people would rather be slapped and have done, than be slapped and fawned on by turns.)

Einstein's Monsters is a book of stories preceded by an introduction, 'Thinkability', in which Martin Amis gives expression to his anti-nuclearism. I say *his* anti-nuclearism, because there is no standard form of opposition to nuclear weapons. You can for instance be against nuclear weapons and in favour of nuclear power, you can be against nuclear weapons and against unilateral disarmament. It is in the negotiation of those *and*s that things get ticklish.

Amis attributes the dawning of his interest in nuclear issues, in 1984, to two distinct stimuli: 'impending fatherhood' and a tardy reading of Jonathan Schell's *The Fate of the Earth*. He doesn't elaborate. But to contemplate, while waiting to become a father, the nature of the world into which a child will be born, though a common experience, is not exactly a logical procedure. The time to reach conclusions about the world, to decide whether it should be asked to bear the weight of another creature – or alternatively whether it can be trusted with a precious new person – was before conception, not before birth.

But there is in fact a deeper logic. Motherhood is a fact, while fatherhood is a fiction, perhaps the first fiction. There are women who have not suspected their pregnancy until some way into labour – even if in such cases it is a matter presumably of awareness blocked, rather than true ignorance – but no women who have become parents, as men can easily do, unawares. For the great majority of women, the physical and mental processes of prospective parenthood go hand in hand, while in men they are necessarily disjunct. Pregnancy has a huge prestige, but the corresponding period in the life of a father-to-be not only has no prestige, but no name.

But though conditional on the acknowledgement of a pregnancy, this period is a quite separate thing, of which women have no experience. In this period a man constructs the persona of the father, jettisoning some aspects of earlier selves and rehabilitating others long disclaimed. New material can be taken on, now that there is a place for it. The whole process may amount only to the displaying of a *Baby on Board* bumpersticker on a car being driven with an unchanged recklessness – though a recklessness suddenly righteous – or it may be profound.

The essay 'Thinkability' is a rhetorical construction, its logic local rather than overarching. Amis states that we must 'find the logic of unanimity', but there is a striking lack of unanimity about the essay. Here for instance is a lovely lyric: '. . . we do not need the econauts of Greenpeace or *The Tao of Physics* to tell us that in our biosphere everything is to do with everything else. In that they are human, all human beings feel it – the balance, the delicacy. We have only one planet, and it is *round*.' And three pages later: 'If we could look at ourselves from anything approaching the vantage of cosmic time, if we had any sense of cosmic power, cosmic delicacy, then every indicator would point the same way: *down*.' The nearest to a syllogism that can be made of these elements is this: All human beings feel the cosmic delicacy. We have no sense of cosmic delicacy. Therefore we are not human beings – which has a strangely unhelpful feel to it.

More worrying than these contradictory flourishes is Amis' tendency to allow in a privileged context arguments that he would resist elsewhere. When he refers to 'the babies who will never be born' if nuclear weapons destroy the world, 'those that are queuing up in spectral relays until the end of time,' he beefs up the rhetoric admirably, but he would hardly appreciate it if the notion of reproachful, non-existent babies hungering for life was to fall into the wrong hands, say the hands of a born-again Christian.

Above all, Martin Amis rejects his own suggestion that 'in our biosphere everything is to do with everything else.' He considers nuclear weapons as an issue in isolation, when in fact this question contains all others only in the limited sense that failure here destroys everything everywhere. As Martin Amis expounds it, the issue of nuclear weapons is an issue without edges, but it is still a single issue. Environmental considerations, for instance, get a look-in only with specific reference to the prospect of a nuclear winter ('the chemistry of ozone creation and destruction . . . is only partially understood'), as if apart from our gaffe of bringing nuclear weapons into being our relationship with the planet was going swimmingly, with bags of respect on both sides.

Amis hives off the issue of nuclear weapons intellectually from other subjects, but he also isolates the nuclear age historically from everything that came before. Nothing is as it was. This rhetorical construction of a Before and an After with nothing in common has the paradoxical effect of elevating the Bomb above history. The Bomb becomes something like the Uncaused Cause of theology. But it is only in its consequences that the Bomb is absolute: to imagine that the development of the Bomb corresponds to no long-standing ingredient of human nature is wishful thinking. The Bomb need never have been invented, but that doesn't make it a visitation.

Martin Amis announces early on in his essay that he doesn't know what to do about nuclear weapons, but he presumably doesn't intend the curious passivity that underlies the habitual agitation of his prose. It can sometimes seem as if equality under the Bomb is the first and last right of man in the nuclear age. The narrator of the story 'Bujak and the Strong Force' asks, in words that could have been transposed from 'Thinkability': 'Gratuitous or recreational crimes of violence, the ever-less-tacit totalitarianism of money ... the pornographic proliferation, the nuclear collapse of the family ... the sappings and distortions of a mediated reality, the sexual abuse of the very old and the very young (of the weak, the weak): what is the hidden denominator here, and what could explain it all?' If the Bomb underlies everything, and we can't do anything about the Bomb, then we can't do anything about anything. But seeking a single explanation for complex phenomena comes perilously close to being a confession of failure in any age.

In this context, as Amis acknowledges, 'questions of decorum present themselves with a force not found elsewhere.' But a certain amount of ingrained, reflexive indecorousness needs to be faced up to. We are always reluctant to admit that our most abstract speculations carry in suspension a silt of self-interest, and we have a particular taboo in this area. Surely, when we talk about Armageddon, we speak from our full humanity – not as men and women with axes to grind, but as people facing an axe as big as the world? We find it painful to admit that even here short-term thinking is our natural mode, so that we must force ourselves towards the sane perspectives.

But in fact this is an area where selfish distortion is more rather than less likely. Since someone who is authentically 'for' nuclear weapons is hard to find, the argument tends to be invisibly controlled, not by what

7

we mutually oppose, but by what we individually seek to maintain.

These days the moral high ground can be claimed by just about anyone, and the ability to decode the real messages under the false has become one of the routine self-defensive skills of modern life. When a prime minister espouses environmental issues almost from one minute to the next, it isn't difficult to locate the disguised agenda – in this case a commitment to nuclear power – the ideology that lies unchanged at the heart of the turnaround. And when an acclaimed novelist, much admired for his cultivated scabrous cynicism, announces a concern for huge issues, or for one huge issue, the question should still be asked: what territory is being defended, consciously or unconsciously, by these manoeuvres?

With Martin Amis, the answer has to be the sexual status quo. His anti-nuclearism is conspicuously male: 'In this debate, we are all arguing with our fathers,' he writes, and the 'we' who are doing the arguing seem very much to be men. The essay 'Thinkability' makes no reference, for instance, to the most single-minded demonstration of nuclear protest, the Peace Camp at Greenham Common, or the larger movement of which it was part. The Peace Camp may have been only a symbolic gesture, but rather less symbolic than an essay, and the language of unanimity would be more eloquent if it registered the contribution of both genders.

At one point Martin Amis writes that nuclear weapons make him feel 'as if a child of mine has been out too long, much too long, and already it is getting dark.' The same sentiment, if it had appeared ten years ago in a book published by the Women's Press, or even been expressed late on at a party in the same period, would not have had a particularly easy reception from Amis as reviewer or fellow-guest.

But the persona of the father is a liberating construction, allowing for the safe expression of emotion in unprecedented quantities (the keyword here is *safe*) – provided it is bounced off children and not expressed direct. Men, moreover, have a freer hand in their rhetorical self-portraits than women, precisely because women are likely to be tied as a matter of day-by-day routine to the small people who are the basis and focus of the changed persona. (Those men who raise children tend to inhabit an aura of specialness, making ordinary things extraordinary by choosing to do them.) A man's children can be his property one minute, and his virtue the next.

As reported in 'Thinkability', the arguments between Kingsley and Martin Amis tail away as the two of them admire Martin's infant son, who will perhaps in time – Martin speculates – come up with a radical solution to the problem of nuclear weapons. Kingsley will have to die off, and so perhaps will Martin. But this imagined radicalism doesn't disturb the structure of patriarchy, which can more easily accommodate parricide than, say, the weakness of listening to your mother, sister, daughter, wife.

Clearly Martin Amis didn't choose to have sons instead of daughters; but if he were a father of daughters his rhetoric would be harder to sustain in its present form. He did, on the other hand, choose to marry, and it is also a matter of choice – literary choice this time – whether he presents himself in 'Thinkability' as husband and father, or just as father. Fatherhood in 'Thinkability' is a lonely responsibility, not an unobtrusive domestic fact, perhaps because on some primitive level children are an overflow of strength, while a wife is an admission of masculine insufficiency.

In fact the only reference to the author's having a wife as well as sons (and a father) is in his nightmare vision of having to travel through the firestorm from the flat where he works to his home, and then to kill her as well as them. Mrs Amis features in the essay only as one more mouth to stop.

The arguments of 'Thinkability' present nuclear weapons as an aberration, albeit the defining aberration of the modern world. There is no suggestion that anything about nuclear weapons corresponds to anything in the world before them, nor to anything profound in the world they hold to ransom.

But a century that saw Auschwitz and Dresden before Hiroshima can hardly claim to be taken aback by technological destruction on a vast scale. It isn't a parvenu principle of our culture that we do things, not because we should, but because we can.

This is not the logic that Martin Amis chooses to pursue, perhaps for fear of ending up on the wrong side of it. The feminist watchword that the personal is political is no longer in its first youth, and has kept some strange old company, but it still has a certain reproachful power, and any approximation to it in 'Thinkability' might crack open the vast latent ironies behind *Einstein's Monsters*.

The nearest that Amis comes to this is a paragraph about the regressive imagery of the Manhattan Project: 'the first bomb . . . was winched up into position on a contraption known as "the cradle"; during the countdown the Los Alamos radio station broadcast a lullaby . . . scientists speculated whether the Gadget was going to be a "girl" (i.e. a dud) or a "boy" (i.e. a device that might obliterate New Mexico). The Hiroshima bomb was called Little Boy. "It's a boy!" pronounced Edward Teller, the "father" of the H-bomb, when "Mike" ("my baby") was detonated over Bikini Atoll in 1952 . . . It is ironic, because *they* are the little boys; *we* are the little boys.' The emphasis that Amis places on the distinction adult/child draws attention away from the distinction male/female, where he isn't on such safe ground himself.

The notion that the entrenched destructiveness of our culture has something to do with the jealously defended imbalance between its sexes finds a place in *Einstein's Monsters* only in an inverted form. Bujak, in the story 'Bujak and the Strong Force', seeing gay punks in the street, interprets 'their plight, and their profusion, as an einsteinian matter also.' The idea seems to be that such violations of the sexual order stem inevitably from the Bomb's disturbing of cosmic balance. Presumably, then, in a world without the Bomb sexual roles would be properly harmonious. This, of course, is only a passing remark made by a fictional character, but there is an absence of characters who take any sort of opposing tack.

In the story 'The Little Puppy That Could', Amis imagines a post-holocaustal future where the sexual status quo has been deformed and distorted along with everything else. Men have become interchangeable – Tim and Tam and Tom – subject to the rule of monstrous matriarchs who, horribly, demand to be pleasured. Now that fertility is a scarce commodity, the world is held to ransom by a womb and not a penis. The women are given names (Keithette, Clivonne, Kevinia) whose ludicrousness may be meant to derive from the supposed laughter-quotient of the male names on which they are based, but there is a definite edge of hysteria to the humour. What seems to bring out the rancour which the comedy disguises, at least from its author, is the very idea of women with male privileges.

At the end of the story the heroine, the intensely feminine Andromeda, has found herself a real man (a transformed puppy, innocent animal purified by fire): 'His arms were strong and warlike as he turned and led her into the cool night. They stood together on the hilltop and gazed down at their new world.' The logic here is arsy-versy, but consistent with the rest of the book's theorising. The Bomb has made men effeminate and women repellently assertive. Now a proper polarisation of the sexes will make possible some sort of renewal.

A feminist suggestion might rather be that it was a

world in thrall to a distorted male identity that made the Bomb in the first place. It seems unlikely that Martin Amis is unaware of this line of thinking. What seems to be at work, here and elsewhere in *Einstein's Monsters*, is *disavowal*, that useful psychological word that means denying something without mentioning it.

The great irony of *Einstein's Monsters* is that a book dedicated to the unapproachable ideal of disarmament should be written by someone so opposed by temperament to disarmament outside the nuclear arena. Martin Amis' progress has been not so much a career as an escalation, the persona increasingly truculent, the style ever more bristling. His very method is overkill. There seems little doubt that in the silos of his notebooks there are stored enough explosive phrases to account for his readers many times over. Though Amis in 'Thinkability' may find the idea baffling, any reader of a page of his mature prose has a pretty good idea of what might be meant by *retaliating first*.

These analogies aren't flippant. Amis himself, despite his remarks about the need for 'decorum' in nuclear discussion, feels free to use the vocabulary of holocaust figuratively. In 'Bujak and the Strong Force' alone, a man who is sensitive to potential violence is said to have a 'fallout detector', Bujak's fist is said to be 'neutronium', to kill a whole family is to 'nuke' them – perhaps to compensate for the nuclear preoccupations in the story seeming rather arbitrarily imposed on its plot. The story of a man whose family is murdered but who takes no revenge could be expressed in terms of the Old Testament giving way to the New, rather than deterrence unilaterally abandoned, but once you've used a nuclear vocabulary it's hard to go back to a conventional one. As the proliferation of nuclear images indicates, whether they are an integral part of the story or not, Amis concentrates on the way the big world infiltrates and corrodes private lives, rather than the other aspect of the traffic, the elusive way that individual behaviour subtends the status quo.

The aggressiveness of Martin Amis' style is of course artificial; it shapes its own highly contrived version of strength and weakness. The monstrous women in 'The Little Puppy That Could' are announced as all-powerful, but are relegated to the role of comic bit-players. The narrator of 'Bujak and the Strong Force', by contrast, is weak, but insistently, buttonholingly, Woody Allenishly weak, and – naturally enough, being the narrator – has control of the point of view, the true seat of power in a story. The hyperbolic phrases Amis gives him promote every flinch into a stylistic swagger, every whimper into a growl.

But if aggressiveness in a style does not correspond to aggressiveness in the world, it does correspond to the power of will. No other aspect of writing responds to pure willpower: sit down at a desk for four hours and you can't guarantee to come up with four satisfactory plot twists or nine convincing insights into character. But you can be pretty sure of coming up with twenty startling images or striking turns of phrase.

Even when Martin Amis is treading water he breaks the surface so much it looks like a shark attack.

A style like Martin Amis' represents both a fear and a desire. It represents a radical doubt about the business of writing, an authorial identity crisis that can be postponed by having each sentence declare the presence of the author. Amis' narrators don't venture abroad without a suit, a shield, without a testudo of style to protect them. Here for instance are three of his narrators, the weak writer from 'Bujak', a disturbed pre-adolescent ('Insight at Flame Lake') and a citizen of the year 2020 ('The Time Disease'), all deploying one of Amis' favourite tropes, the cadenced triptych of synonyms:

'If the world disarmed tomorrow, he believed, the species would still need at least a century of recuperation, after its entanglement, its flirtation, after its thing with the strong force.'

'Meanwhile I stare into the brilliance and burnish, into the mauve of the MIRVed lake.'

'Up there in the blasted, the totalled, up there in the fucked sky.'

Fear of inauthenticity here leads to inauthenticity of a different sort, not an unsigned painting but a painting composed entirely of signatures. The reader who is reminded by each succeeding sentence of the looming designs of the author is denied much of the traditional pleasure of literature, the pleasure of surrendering to an imagined world rather than being bullied into finding it impressive. The supposed opposition between highly-wrought and unambitious ways of writing on which Amis' style depends doesn't hold up in any case. There is writing which advertises its surprises and writing that simply springs them. Eudora Welty, for instance, when she writes a sly sentence like 'The librarian was the lady in town who wanted to be it,' makes no obviously odd choices, but doesn't on that account go short of sleights and syncopations.

It is this absence of a neutral register from Martin Amis' work, oddly enough, that his father Kingsley complains of, the lack of workaday sentences not hell-bent on shock or charm. Here and there in *Einstein's Monsters* Amis hides his hand and aspires to such transparency, notably in the story 'Insight at Flame Lake', which alternates two diaries, of a disturbed pre-adolescent and his uncomprehending uncle. But all it takes is one electric adjective too many and the jig is up, the familiar antagonistic persona reaches criticality.

The other aspect of a style like Martin Amis' is the desire to make a mark at all costs – not the strongest basis from which to mount an attack on the moral blindnesses of the nuclear age. It is noticeable for instance that in 'Thinkability' he has a shot at rendering nuclear war in his particular tone of voice, in a sentence that ends with the distinctive juxtaposition 'the warped atoms, the grovelling dead.' Forget the ambition of finding the language of unanimity: this is a holocaust with a monogram, almost a copyright logo.

The military analogies are irresistible, though the ugly sound you hear is only the dull clang of polemic against polemic. Martin Amis' anti-nuclear stance is in the nature of a pre-emptive strike, detonating an issue that might otherwise be used against him. A woman's hand on the button, after all, would do far more damage to his world-view. By striking first, he can cut the supply lines between the nuclear issue and other issues he doesn't want to engage with: feminism and environmentalism, half of humanity and the whole of its home.

In Amis' new novel, *London Fields*, there is a broadened concern with the whole degraded planet. But there is also an incongruous gleeful pessimism, a rush of satisfaction at making things as bad as they can possibly be. Amis is still in the business of making elegant terminal diagnoses, and has no interest in cures.

But there are other ways of engaging with the nuclear issue. To turn briefly to another writer who started his career as a bad boy and has metamorphosed into a good father: Ian McEwan's anti-nuclearism offers a useful contrast to Martin Amis', in that he knows at least in general terms what to do about nuclear weapons. The crucial line of his anti-nuclear oratorio, after all, is 'Shall there be womanly times, or shall we die?' It isn't clear whether the phrase 'womanly times' invokes power for women or a less rigid identity for men – and the difference, believe it or not, is crucial. And of course the actual mechanism of change is unclear. The Maharishi Mahesh Yogi used to advertise classes in transcendental meditation with claims that the crime rate would plummet once

10 per cent of the population started to meditate regularly. It may be that in Ian McEwan's vision of things, a society where a true relation between the sexes exists cannot – in a similarly impalpable but effective way – sustain an impulse of destruction.

For McEwan, feminism and anti-nuclearism are inseparable: but for Amis, anti-nuclearism is actually a substitute for feminism, performing the same rhetorical function of disengaging him from human destructiveness. But it is a rhetoric deeply suspect and divided. By saying a mighty No, in the voice that his sons lend him, to the nuclear negation, he aligns himself with life without actually saying Yes to anything, or committing himself to any sort of change below the superpower level.

But I don't at all mean that Martin Amis should break his pencil, and short the circuits of his word processor with the tears of his remorse. Quite the reverse. It is actually his need for absolution in the modern manner, surfacing most plainly in *Einstein's Monsters*, that threatens his stature as a writer.

Our culture is currently in the throes of a mania for self-exoneration. In every newspaper, polluting industries advertise themselves clean; the most compromised public figures somehow find their way to the high moral ground. If mere reality was as easily satisfied with gestures and good intentions as we are, there would be nothing much wrong with the world. But failing that, we have some dim obligation to treat things as they are, and not to join the stampede towards a fashionable innocence. Although writers may be on the side of the angels, they don't get to be that way by awarding themselves wings.

But already in Amis' *Money* there was the extraordinary move of including a character called Martin Amis, for fear that the reader might identify the author with his monstrous creation John Self. The resulting loss of tension would be disastrous for a less energetic book. It's not the case that a persona is a self-portrait unless the author testifies to the contrary, but nor are the ingredients for its making gathered on the Mountains of the Moon. There is a relationship, however shifting and elusive, between author and mask, and to announce their absolute separateness is to limit the power of each. The attraction for Martin Amis of the things he wants to dislike – a category that includes any number of impure appetites, sexual, social and even political – is actually the great subject of his work, a troubling burden he is the poorer for casting off.

Ian McEwan's *The Child in Time* may be the most sustained meditation on paternity in literature. It treats fatherhood, though, not as an experience – the hero's daughter is missing for the vast majority of the book – but as a condition. For the hero, Stephen Lewis, fatherhood is not a crude fact of biography but an irreversible existential state, not dependent on a current relationship with a present child.

The Child in Time is set in 1996, and flashes back two years to the abduction of Kate, then aged three. The novel doesn't spell out the year of its setting: I mention it here, perversely enough, to demonstrate that I can be true to a text when I want to, that I still have some residual power to read a text along the grain, rather than against it. The present tense of the book is set in a year of Olympic Games – which restricts the possibilities to the series 1992, 1996, 2000 . . . The year also contains what turns out to be 'the last decent summer of the twentieth century', a formula which disposes of the third of these candidates. As between 1992 and 1996 the evidence is softer, less definite. But if two years before, at the time of Kate's disappearance, Stephen is reassured rather than made uneasy by the 'oil and leather smell' of the gunbelts worn by policemen on routine duties, it seems reasonable to assume enough time from the date of writing not only for the necessary legislation, but for psychological adaptation on the part of the citizenry. The earlier date hardly leaves space for these legal and social changes.

1996, then. Two years earlier, Stephen takes Kate shopping, leaving his wife Julie to sleep. He returns alone; someone has abducted Kate in the supermarket, and her parents never see her again. But the actual circumstances of the disappearance are curiously unconvincing, as most readers of the book have acknowledged. (That is a flat lie – I know of no one who was even faintly troubled by the passage – but critics get lonely too.)

The difficulty is that Kate is taken while actually holding on to the supermarket trolley Stephen is unloading, in the tiny interval between his asking for a carrier bag and receiving it. Now, clearly you could draw a graph of abductions that plotted likelihood against culpability. In the case of a child, for instance, left in a trolley in the supermarket parking lot over a Bank Holiday weekend, the likelihood of her being taken would be high, the culpability of whoever had left her there also high. If on the other hand a master-criminal contrived to abduct Kate while Stephen was walking with her down the street, so that he noticed nothing until he glanced down and saw he was holding a small artificial hand, cunningly weighted, in a brightly-coloured glove, why, that would have a very low culpability rating – what parent can guard against that sort of ruse? – but likewise a likelihood vanishingly small.

What McEwan has contrived in his book is very much towards the master-criminal end of the scale. It's highly improbable that a child could be snatched in this way unobserved; but if an experienced author chooses to present his material in this way, it must be because the compensations seem to him to be worth it. In other words, it is less important to him to be plausible than to defend a fictional father against accusations of negligence. The image and priorities of the father are paramount, and this sets a pattern for the book. That is both what it assumes and what it sets out to prove.

A moment that tends to confirm this follows almost immediately. As the alarm spreads through the supermarket, and the search moves to the street, male members of staff are suddenly 'no longer warehouse-men or sub-managers or company representatives, but fathers, potential or real.' It's odd that fatherhood, potential or real, should be regarded as the precondition for human feeling, as if there was no other possible basis for emotion in a man. But at least *The Child in Time* is consistent in conflating fatherhood and humanity. It's ironic that McEwan, hardly a Thatcherite, should use the tactic, familiar from governmental rhetoric of recent years, of defining a universal experience in slyly narrow terms, though in this case the substitution is of 'father' for 'man' rather than, say, 'active citizen' for 'citizen'.

But why do men become fathers? How – psychologically – do they become fathers? On these subjects, rather surprisingly, *The Child in Time* has nothing to say. Stephen's early life with Julie before they are parents, the pivotal period, is passed over. Fatherhood is assumed, without its even being mentioned, to be the male destiny, though Stephen is also privileged in the novel by not having any rivals, as if he was the only father in the world.

But in order to boost the option of fatherhood, still without mentioning it, other career possibilities for men are made to seem casual and contingent. Stephen becomes an author of children's books more or less by accident, and Charles Darke, first his publisher and then his friend, embarks on a high-flying political career after all but tossing a coin to decide his choice of party. When men's jobs are such arbitrary excursions into the world, paternity is bound to seem a thing of purposeful integrity, without needing to be addressed directly.

As for Stephen's partner in parenthood: Julie becomes estranged from him, when the paths of their mourning diverge. In due course she moves out, and settles in a cottage in the country. For the bulk of the book, Stephen deals with solitude or with his parents, either biological or symbolic (Charles Darke and his wife Thelma). But before Julie leaves comes a sentence with a faint jarring note: 'He suspected – and it turned out later he was correct – that she took his efforts to be a typically masculine evasion, an attempt to mask feelings behind displays of competence and organisation and physical effort.' The oddity is the clause between dashes. It isn't usual for McEwan to compromise his chosen point of view in this way, a formal puncturing even when the intention, as here, is to reinforce with corroboration. But it seems that even in a book that pays as careful a lip-service to women's perceptions as this one, male priorities must be defended. Men get points, not for changing, but for being right about women thinking they are wrong.

In his dealings with his biological parents Stephen is, not surprisingly given their relative times of life, tender and solicitous, protective of their reflex to protect him. At one moment he all but tucks them in for the night.

But Ian McEwan isn't content with the ordinary reversals that time visits on relationships. He contrives for his hero Stephen a paranormal experience, in which he is present, looking through a pub window, when his mother decides to defy Stephen's father and bring to term the pregnancy that will be Stephen. The experience is presented from Stephen's point of view as acutely distressing: 'His eyes grew large and round and lidless with desperate, protesting innocence, his knees rose under him and touched his chin, his fingers were scaly flippers, gills beat time, urgent, helpless strokes through the salty ocean . . .' But this is only an example of the book's strategy of taking one small step backwards and several big strides forward; the bolder the novel's advance, the more it is disguised with artificial shrinkings. Mrs Lewis when she corroborates Stephen's vision testifies to the power of the white and pleading face she sees through the window. It enables her to establish a relationship with her future child, and to defeat the forces ranged against this precarious but resourceful being. Stephen is not only present at this crucial moment, he intervenes in it. He creates himself. This is to extend the fantasy of paternity pretty far, with Stephen becoming in effect his own father, and overruling the wishes of his biological father to boot.

In the scenes of Stephen's vision, and its subsequent confirmation by his mother, the fantasy that underlies the whole book is uncomfortably naked. It becomes rather too evident that the desires of a man so taken up with the processes and privileges of reproduction actually move towards doing without women, or certainly minimising their part in the creation of life.

The nearest, by contrast, that the book comes to acknowledging that fathers can be manipulative, even destructive, is in its portrayal of Charles Darke, whose paternity is of course purely symbolic. Darke publishes Stephen's novel *Lemonade* and makes him famous, but exacts the price that it is marketed (not at all Stephen's intention) as a children's book. Darke promotes him in a way that is also a demotion, both making and unmaking him as a man. There is a similar pattern to Stephen's involvement in an Official Commission on Childcare – he is only appointed to it through Charles Darke's influence, but Darke also writes the unofficial document which pre-empts the Committee's work and makes its conclusions irrelevant. Darke gives, and Darke takes away.

But Darke is not a real father, and his sponsorship of Stephen is a manipulative perversion of the real thing. The conclusion of the novel's Darke-strand is that men who do not produce children are condemned to become them. Charles Darke produces a guide to childcare that is oppressively authoritarian, but himself longs to return to an infantile irresponsibility. In the novel, he gets to realise this fantasy, in a way that leads to his death. He becomes a failed and futureless child.

Each chapter of *The Child in Time* is headed by a passage from *The Authorised Childcare Handbook*, the volume written by Charles Darke. Darke functions in the book as a whole as a decoy, making Stephen's version of masculinity seem natural by the contrast with his highly unstable overcompensations, but the extracts from his book play an even more useful distracting role. They enable McEwan to conjure up a world in which the family is under threat from outside forces, so that the greater part of the book's energy can in fact be devoted to reshaping it from within.

However much the world has changed around Ian McEwan in the years since he started writing, it seems fair to say that he has changed more. In his early stories the only rule about sex seemed to be that it should *not* take place, with marital commitment and reproductive intent, within a fertile cleft – and the further removed it was from that situation the more it seemed to interest him. It would be hard to extrapolate this state of affairs backwards from *The Child in Time*, now that desire has been so completely mortgaged to the creation of new life. To read McEwan's novels in order, from the fixated adolescents of *The Cement Garden* through the drily passionate couple, childless and solipsistic, of *The Comfort of Strangers*, to the exemplary carers of *The Child in Time*, is to trace a drastic retraction of libido. (His new novel *The Innocent* seems to acknowledge that this progression has reached a dead end by starting again with virginity and romantic love.)

But it would be as much of a mistake to exaggerate the distance this author has travelled as to ignore it. Just as McEwan's early stories contained an element of artificial perversity, so *The Child in Time* conceals within it, for all its emphasis on universal experiences of love and loss, a fierce private agenda. There is a strong paradoxical thread leading from the apparent, but perhaps misleading, coldness of his early work and the apparent, but perhaps also misleading, warmth of the maturity announced by *The Child in Time*.

Charles Darke's wife delivers the verdict on her husband that his case '"was just an extreme form of a general problem"', men's inability to carry over the virtues of their immaturity into adulthood. Stephen agrees with this argument, and Thelma Darke then briefly turns it against him, saying that his indulgence of his emotions since Kate's disappearance has been a form of wilful blindness, and moreover a refusal of knowledge.

This fleeting indictment has a certain amount of authority, since by gender and profession Thelma unites the novel's two strongest images of a mutability profounder than the established order: femininity and the new physics. But it is the last of Stephen's ordeals before the novel gives him his reward. It will be everything he dreamed of.

The procedures of *The Child in Time* are intensely 'feminine', as men tend to use that word, indirect and dissembling, making each fresh inroad seem like a retreat. But now the book moves up a number of gears, from deferent advances to submissive annexation. McEwan mounts an extraordinarily daring raid on the very citadel of fertility. In the last, closely written scene of the book, Stephen attends the birth of a child he did not even know Julie was expecting. (The couple have hardly communicated since Stephen's visit to the country during which the child was conceived, the same visit that gave him his vision of his parents.)

The Child in Time is a narrative of pain and loss, but it is also a suppressed drama of symbolic owner-

ship. The irony of its construction is that the disappearance of Kate makes the claims of her parents
artificially equal. Only in the absence of the child does
it become possible for the father's claims to be heard
so favourably. The missing daughter becomes common property, and Stephen's feelings can dominate
the novel.

Consequently, when Stephen finds Julie close to
term, her pregnancy – suddenly looming, without
preparation – seems more than anything an objective
correlative to the development Stephen has under-
gone during the novel. But he receives more gifts
from the fiction he inhabits than that. He and Julie
make love, and their love-making flows into, if it
doesn't actually trigger, the birth.

A little earlier, on his way to see Julie, Stephen has
fulfilled his boyhood dream of riding in the cab of a
railway engine. Now the older dream that haunts the
book, of a man playing an immediate part not just
in conception but in birth, has its fulfilment too,
accompanied by a full-throated lyric: 'The silence
resounded after all their promises, and merged with
the stirring of a billion needles in the plantation. He
moved inside her gently. Something was gathering up
around them, growing louder, tasting sweeter, getting
warmer, brighter, all senses were synthesising, con-
densing in the idea of increase.'

Stephen must forfeit this feeling of inclusion once
Julie's labour gets fully under way. He falls back on
the learned routines of the labour partner, though he
feels that the basic purpose of such routines is 'to

oppose the panic of paternal helplessness'. But on this occasion, unlike the last, his help will be all-important, since there is no one else around.

He casts his mind back to the time of Julie's first confinement. 'He had been brow mopper, telephonist, flower man, champagne pourer, midwife's dogsbody, and he had talked her through. Afterwards she had told him he had been useful. His impression was that his value had been more symbolic.' This could almost be the crux of the novel: the male exclusion, endlessly worried at and compensated for, from the reality of creation.

After all, no reason of any kind is given in the novel for the disappearance of Kate. There is no suspect and no motive, though on the naturalistic level many children would be easier to make off with than this particular one, loved and supervised, holding on to her father's supermarket trolley. Even on the symbolic level, there is nothing that her parents do, or fail to do, that would make them unworthy of her continued existence. The whole book resonates with Kate's absence, but into that resonating space is dropped only one infinitesimal suggestion of imperfection, which hangs in the mind only because it has no competitors: Stephen's role in her birth was only symbolic. Kate was fully mothered, but was only imperfectly fathered. There was an imbalance at the very moment of her coming into being.

If this was a flaw in the making of her, the Lewises' second child will not suffer from it. Stephen telephones the midwife, but until she arrives he must stand in for her. In fact the Lewises are parents again, and the action of the book is over, before she arrives.

Lifting the sheet clear on Julie's orders, Stephen sees, to his shock, 'a presence, a revelation': the baby's protruding head. It is silent and still. He can detect no pulse or breath. When he touches the head, he can feel a warmth of sorts, but it is too faint, and fading, a warmth borrowed from Julie's body. He is abruptly comforted by 'a memory, brief and clear like a firework, of a sunlit country road, of wreckage and a head.' This is another crucial elusive sentence, disguised by its brevity, its incongruity, and its being followed so closely by a sentence fuller of obvious significance, the trumpeted meaning of a novel's closing pages: 'This is really all we have got, this increase, this matter of life loving itself, everything we have has to come from this.'

The memory-firework flashes back to an incident when Stephen was driving down to the Darkes' country house. A lorry overturned in front of his car, and he escaped injury only by some inspired driving, aiming the vehicle into an impossibly narrow gap. Lightheaded in the aftermath of the crash, he tries to find the driver in the wreckage of the cab. He hears a voice, repeating a brief verbal formula, but can't locate the speaker. Then he hears that the words are in fact 'Look down.' He does.

There is a head at his feet, and an arm pressed into the face, obscuring the mouth. The man appears to be badly hurt, unable to feel anything below the neck, but eventually Stephen manages, with the help of a jack from his car, to deliver him from the wreckage. His injuries are in fact trifling.

Even on an innocent first reading, if you can imagine such a thing, there seems to be something slyly obstetrical about Stephen's handiwork with the jack. But the analogy becomes sharper and much more purposeful when the reader is referred back to it by the unemphatic sentence from the book's last scene. Although the compressed wreckage is compared to a tightly closed fist, or a toothless mouth held shut, a different anatomical suggestion is made when Stephen sees the driver's head protruding from 'a vertical gash in the steel'.

A writer as careful as Ian McEwan doesn't use a piece of taboo slang by accident, but the pun that depends on it is well disguised by its context. As that scurrilous, or mischievous, but certainly not neutral 'gash' indicates, this passage gives expression to a negative imagery of childbirth, to what Melanie Klein might have termed the Bad Womb rather than the Good. A man may think of childbirth as a mystery, as an apotheosis, or simply as an enviable power; or he may think of it as a piece of indifferent machinery, a bleeding trap, even an atrocity. This passage represents the second set of images, disavowed elsewhere in this determinedly feminism-friendly novel, tolerated here only in disguise and at some considerable distance from an appropriate context – as a gentle child might disfigure a doll and bury it far from the house.

Back to the nativity scene. In the light of the

31

memory-firework, Stephen sees what he must do. He reaches into the wreckage and finds the umbilical cord, which is wound twice round the baby's neck and is already well on the way to strangling it. He works the cord clear, and as he does so Julie gives birth.

So it is that the hero of *The Child in Time* plays as decisive a role in the birth of his second child as he did, elsewhere in the book, in his own viability as a foetus. Twenty-five pages earlier, in a railway station, he has given his coat to a beggar, and this hint of Christliness has been admirably developed since then. Julie's baby was as cold and still as Lazarus, until he called it forth from the shadows.

In 1989 *The Child in Time* was a featured title in a festival of Green books, on the basis that it called for a more nurturing relationship with the environment. That may be true, but it is also true that a few green sprigs can be used to brighten up almost any ideology. Ian McEwan may be one of the few successful literary examples of the New Man (there it is, the dreaded phrase at last), but in his vision of the relationship between the sexes there is much that is atavistic, patriarchal, even patristic. It was an idea of the Early Fathers of the Church, after all, following Aristotle, that woman was responsible only for the body of a child, man for the soul. Woman the factory of flesh, man the author of breath, as Stephen is so literally. On this reading of fatherhood, maternity is brute and gross, paternity spiritual, and the men have nothing to envy.

Only in the last sentence of *The Child in Time* do the new parents think to discover the sex of their infant. They are described, as Julie reaches under the covers to find out, as being about to rejoin the world – the world by implication of definition, of fixity. But the reader has learned to be just a little suspicious by now of the contrived preceding flux: not a true indifference to gender, let alone a transcendence of it, but a temporary artificial blurring of identities, under cover of which the male, all the while loudly extolling the sanctity of her privileges, usurps the female.

Clearly the two writers considered in this essay adopt utterly different attitudes to the problems of the world, and to their places in it. Martin Amis declares a separate war against the Bomb, a private treaty of antagonism, while Ian McEwan tries to smuggle himself across the border of gender. But their situation is similar. Each is seeking to align himself with qualities traditionally associated with women, with a certain tender-mindedness. Each in his own way bears witness to the tidal pull of feminist thinking, and to a nagging doubt about the authenticity of male experience (the Venus Envy of my title).

Anthropologists use the word *couvade* to denote patterns of male behaviour that seek to upstage or to appropriate potent moments in the lives of women. The women go into labour, but the men – it varies from culture to culture – either cry out in stylised agony, or else persuade themselves they actually feel the pangs.

33

There is certainly something poignant about a man seeking to make fatherhood a binding contract, the lynchpin of his identity, at roughly the same time that Angela Carter, newly and maturely a mother, was saying in interview – with splendid defiance of biology – that no one should think of having children until their forties, because at that time of life you don't so much mind giving up your evenings. Angela Carter was trying to find a style of motherhood that was casual, breezy, matter-of-fact – just as fatherhood has traditionally been – while Ian McEwan, and to a lesser extent Martin Amis, was trying to turn fatherhood into an experience as immediate and binding as motherhood has been, on the traditional model.

Presumably these writers will ease up on the paternity motif as their actual children grow up to be more obstreperous, less completely contained by their parents' world, not such handy screens for the projection of masculine emotion. Fathers of teenagers lose the habit of wearing paternity as a medal. Till then, it would be refreshing if writers were a little more even-handed in their treatment of such material.

If two people decide to have a child, they are doing one thing, not two. It can't be the case that one of them is capitulating to her biology, while the other is making a commitment to the future. Children have no absolute value, and nor do parents, unless people do, full stop. A *Baby on Board* bumpersticker ignores the fact that the children it seeks to defend, if spared an early death on the road, are no less likely than any others to go joyriding in a borrowed car with a snootful of cider the weekend they turn fourteen. You may want to preserve your children, your genetic possessions, but that isn't enough by itself to turn you into a conservationist.

If, above all, a man finds that becoming a father changes his opinions on all manner of related and unrelated subjects, then he shouldn't simply entrench himself in his new status, and the authority it seems to confer. He should also think about *change*, and how it has happened that his view of the world has shifted through 180 degrees, without any admitted inconsistency. One of the bases of sexism has traditionally been an imagery of women as changeable, unreliable, fickle and so on, with a corresponding exaggerated ideology of male fixedness and stability of purpose. This ideology could usefully be renounced, or at least revised, by those who no longer hold it as they did. But in practice, fathers hold tight to their new fixity, and rapidly forget the old one.

The result is a streamlined account of masculinity that leaves out everything disreputable, in a display of presentational skills that might make you wonder if British Man plc isn't being rejigged in the run-up to privatisation. But disreputability has its own story to tell. Alasdair Gray is a writer of an older generation than Martin Amis and Ian McEwan, with less sophisticated reflexes on issues of sexual politics, and in his 1984 novel *1982, Janine* he concentrates almost exclusively on the disreputable, telling the story of a Scottish supervisor of security installations fantasising in a hotel bedroom. The fantasies are intricate, and constantly threaten to be unforgivable, though Gray knows just how to rehabilitate the fantasist with humour, at the very moment when the reader is poised to reject him. The fantasies all concern having sexual and physical power over women. And then, after nearly 200 pages, Gray makes his move, in one of the most audacious passages in modern British literature:

'. . . I had started to tell myself stories about a very free attractive greedy woman who, confident in her powers, begins an exciting adventure and finds she is not free at all but completely at the disposal of others. As I aged that story became very elaborate. The woman is corrupted into enjoying her bondage and trapping others into it. I did not notice that this was the story of my own life. I avoided doing so by insisting on the *femaleness* of the main character. The parts of the story which came to excite me most were not the physical humiliations but the moment when the trap starts closing and the victim feels the torture of being in two minds: wanting to believe, struggling to believe, that what is happening cannot be happening, can only happen to someone else. And I was right to be excited by that moment because it is the moment when, with courage, we change things. Why *should* Janine feel helpless when she realises Max has lied to her and is abducting her? He is driving a fast car along a motor-way, his hands are occupied, if she removes one of her ridiculous shoes and threatens his eye with the heel he will certainly stop or change direction if he sees she is serious. But she is not used to acting boldly, she finds it easier to pretend Max is honest and decent, hoping her act will make him more so,

36

and thus he drives her into the mire. My fancies keep reliving that moment of torture for Janine because I have never fully faced it in my own life and I am travelling in a circle again.'

This passage finds a new emotion and a new truth in the feminist criticism that when men talk about women they are usually not talking about women at all. Alasdair Gray chooses as his subject the part of the male psyche that is almost by definition the most distorted and destructive, and finds in it, safely encoded, a simple message that has been scrambled everywhere else by the high-minded censors of consciousness. A profound truth has survived by allying itself with the strong unexamined current of sex, and has only been recovered by a willingness to start from the most unprepossessing materials. The more fashionable tendency in British literature is to present masculinity in its more reputable aspects, but it is a tendency, as this essay exists to show, with its own inbuilt drive towards distortion.

But there is a further irony lurking. These late accommodations of feminist ideas are affected by the blowing of quite another wind. Our understanding of the stranglehold we have on our planet has changed, and must change a lot more. The phrase 'doomsday device', once applied specifically to the nuclear arsenals, now seems to cover a much wider range of apparatus: aerosols, fridges, cars. As our fear of national leaders with their fingers on the Button recedes, we must acknowledge that our own hands have been busy, with nozzles and switches and ignition keys. If as Martin Amis suggests it has taken us all this time to learn to write about what uranium can do, how quick will we be to address the issue of carbon dioxide?

In this altered climate, we must learn to accept that our culture suffers from more than a bout of bad breath which some gargle of the future will rid us of. Every time we oust a species or vaporise a habitat we add another clause to the long eviction order we are serving on ourselves. Somehow we must bring together our experience of our lives as meaningful – since without that we will have no motive to improve matters – and our abstract knowledge of their unsustainability.

It will take more than the 'womanly times' prayed for by Ian McEwan to bring this about. In fact it may be that the special and restricted female prestige of recent decades, based on a recognition of women's submerged social and political identity, will suffer in the years to come, rather than sweep the field. It was a powerful piece of rhetoric, after all, on the part of women's peace groups, to characterise the Bomb as inherently masculine, a piece of diabolical machinery that no woman would invent or think of using (tit for tat, this, for the dreary question Why no great female composers?). But if our idea of our destructiveness stops being vested so absolutely in nuclear weapons, and comes to be seen as diffused through all our lives, then female innocence is likely to show up as an illusion. When hairspray and nappy bleach are added to the list of doomsday devices, women may find that the personal is political in a way that no one had quite bargained for.

For a while yet, men of good will and imperfect conscience will try to find an existential niche in the traditional realm of female values. But the phantom of human virtue is set to become still more elusive. The womb cannot survive forever as an innocent organ in a body otherwise discredited. The island of exemption offered by caring for children can only be eaten away, as time passes and the waters rise.

And you, my hobbyhorse, how is it with you? Once or twice I heard the finger-drumming of your gallop, once or twice I thought you would lift me off my feet, while I urged you onwards with my rubber spurs. Let me loosen your girth-straps. Surely that is sweat, darkening the nap of your cheekbone? Your mane lies in lank strands, rinsed by passion of all its chemical bounce. And this foam that trails from your mouth, isn't that the authentic foam of unreason, positively proof that rancorous emotion has achieved its orgasm?

(Bring the camera in close, close as you can. Focus. *Focus!*)

I can only apologise. It appears in fact to be tooth-paste.

About the Author

ADAM MARS-JONES is a writer of fiction (*Lantern Lecture* and *The Darker Proof*, co-written with Edmund White) and the film critic of the *Independent*.

CHATTO
Counter*Blasts*

Also available in bookshops now:-

Forthcoming Chatto Counter*Blasts*

Plus pamphlets from Michael Holroyd, Hanif Kureishi, Michael Ignatieff and Susannah Clapp

If you want to join in the debate, and if you want to know more about **Counter*Blasts***, the writers and the issues, then write to:

Random Century Group, Freepost 5066, Dept MH, London SW1V 2YY